Parenting

Raising Faithful Preschoolers

Augsburg Fortress, Minneapolis

Contents

INTERSECTIONS
Small Group Series

Parenting
Raising Faithful Preschoolers

Developed in cooperation with the Division for Congregational Ministries.

George S. Johnson, series introduction
John Roberto, Center for Ministry Development editor
Leif Kehrwald and Rene Kehrwald, contributors
Laurie J. Hanson and Jill Carroll Lafferty, editors
The Wells Group, series design
Cover photo: © 2001 Visual Images
Page 21 illustration: Brian Jensen/Studio Arts

Materials identified as *LBW* are from *Lutheran Book of Worship*, copyright 1978.

Scripture quotations are from New Revised Standard Version Bible, copyright 1989 Division of Christian Education of the National Council of the Churches of Christ in the United States of America. Used by permission.

1 2 3 4 5 6 7 8 9 0 1 2 3 4 5 6 7 8 9

Introduction

A quick look at the family section of your local bookstore will reveal dozens of books about parenting. What you probably will not find among these titles is a book about parenting and faith growth. *Parenting: Raising Faithful Preschoolers* is specifically designed for parents of preschool children. It provides an understanding of the unique characteristics of young (preschool) children and ideas and strategies for nurturing faith in their lives by sharing Christian values, celebrating rituals, praying together, serving those in need, and developing a strong family life. *Parenting: Raising Faithful Preschoolers* also suggests ways that you can continue growing as you walk with your child in faith.

Family life changes for all time with the entry of an infant into the family. Rooms get reshuffled and family roles redefined. Change becomes a constant in family life as infants become toddlers, and toddlers start to run. Important first lessons about love and forgiveness, right and wrong, are passed on verbally and nonverbally, through actions and through words. The child is shaped by his or her family and reshapes the family in return. Part of that shaping and passing on involves sharing an experience of God and faith life with children. What children learn about faith from parents and family in the first few years of their lives provides a strong foundation for all later teaching and experience.

This book and your small group can give you support and encouragement for growing in faith and raising faithful preschoolers.

Developmental assets

Search Institute, a research and educational organization in Minneapolis, has compiled a list of 40 developmental assets for preschoolers. (See page 52.) These assets are components identified in the lives of healthy, happy, well-adjusted children. They are named in this course as an awareness-raising guide as we work to raise healthy, faithful children.

Baptismal promises

This baptismal symbol appears in each chapter next to activities that remind us of the promises we make when our children are baptized.

SMALL GROUP SERIES

Welcome into the family of those who are part of small groups! Intersections Small Group Series will help you and other members of your group build relationships and discover ways to connect the Christian faith with your everyday life.

This book is prepared for those who want to make a difference in this world, who want to grow in their Christian faith, as well as for those who are beginning to explore the Christian faith. The information in this introduction to the Intersections small-group experience can help your group make the most out of your time together.

Biblical encouragement

Do not be conformed to this world, but be transformed by the renewing of your minds, so that you may discern what is the will of God—what is good and acceptable and perfect. Romans 12:2

Small groups provide an atmosphere where the Holy Spirit can transform lives. As you share your life stories and learn together, God's Spirit can work to enlighten and direct you.

Strength is provided to face the pressures to conform to forces and influences that are opposed to what is "good and acceptable and perfect." To "be transformed" is an ongoing experience of God's grace as we take up the cross and follow Jesus. Changed lives happen as we live in community with one another. Small groups encourage such change and growth.

What is a small group?

A number of definitions and descriptions of the small-group ministry experience exist throughout the church. Roberta Hestenes, a Presbyterian pastor and author, defines a small group as an intentional face-to-face gathering of three to 12 people who meet regularly with the common purpose of discovering and growing in the possibilities of the abundant life.

Whatever definition you use, the following characteristics are important.

Small—Seven to 10 people is ideal so that everyone can be heard and no one's voice is lost. More than 12 members makes genuine caring difficult.

Intentional—Commitment to the group is a high priority.

Personal—Sharing experiences and insights is more important than mastering content.

Conversational—Leaders who facilitate conversation, rather than teach, are the key to encouraging participation.

Friendly—Having a warm, accepting, nonjudgmental atmosphere is essential.

Christ-centered—The small-group experience is biblically based, related to the real world, and founded on Christ.

Features of Intersections Small Group Series

A small-group model

A number of small-group ministry models exist. Most models include three types of small groups:

- *Discipleship groups*—where people gather to grow in Christian faith and life;

- *Support and recovery group*s—which focus on special interests, concerns, or needs; and

- *Ministry groups*—which have a task-oriented focus.

Intersections Small Group Series offers material for all of these.

For discipleship groups, this series offers a variety of courses with Bible study at the center. What makes a discipleship group different from traditional group Bible studies? In discipleship groups, members bring their life experience to the exploration of the biblical material.

For support and recovery groups, Intersections Small Group Series offers topical material to assist group members in dealing with issues related to their common experience, hurt, or interest. An extra section of facilitator helps in the back of the book will assist leaders of support and recovery groups to anticipate and prepare for special circumstances and needs that may arise as group members explore a topic.

Ministry groups can benefit from an environment that includes prayer, biblical reflection, and relationship building, in addition to their task focus.

Four essentials

Prayer, personal sharing, biblical reflection, and a group ministry task are part of each time you gather. These are all important for Christian community to be experienced. Each of the six chapter themes in each book includes:

- Short prayers to open and close your time together.

- Carefully worded questions to make personal sharing safe, nonthreatening, and voluntary.

- A biblical base from which to understand and discover the power and grace of God. God's Word is the compass that keeps the group on course.

- A group ministry task to encourage both individuals and the group as a whole to find ways to put faith into action.

Flexibility

Each book contains six chapter themes that may be covered in six sessions or easily extended for groups that meet for a longer period of time. Each chapter theme is organized around two to three main topics with supplemental material to make it easily adaptable to your small group's needs. You need not use all the material. Most themes will work well for 1½- to 2-hour sessions, but a variety of scheduling options is possible.

Bible-based

Each of the six chapter themes in the book includes one or more Bible texts printed in its entirety from the New Revised Standard Version of the Bible. This makes it easy for all group members to read and learn from the same text. Participants will be encouraged through questions, with exercises, and by other group members to address biblical texts in the context of their own lives.

User-friendly

The material is prepared in such a way that it is easy to follow, practical, and does not require a professional to lead it. Designating one to be the facilitator to guide the group is important, but there is no requirement for this person to be theologically trained or an expert in the course topic. Many times options are given so that no one will feel forced into any set way of responding.

Group goals and process

1. Creating a group covenant or contract for your time together will be important. During your first meeting, discuss these important characteristics of all small groups and decide how your group will handle them.

Confidentiality—Agreeing that sensitive issues that are shared remain in the group.

Regular attendance—Agreeing to make meetings a top priority.

Nonjudgmental behavior—Agreeing to confess one's own shortcomings, if appropriate, not those of others, and not giving advice unless asked for it.

Prayer and support—Being sensitive to one another, listening, becoming a caring community.

Accountability—Being responsible to each other and open to change.

Items in your covenant should be agreed upon by all members. Add to the group covenant as you go along. Space to record key aspects is included in the back of this book. See page 51.

2. Everyone is responsible for the success of the group, but do arrange to have one facilitator who can guide the group process each time you meet.

The facilitator is not a teacher or healer. Teaching, learning, and healing happen from the group experience. The facilitator is more of a shepherd who leads the flock to where they can feed and drink and feel safe.

Remember, an important goal is to experience genuine love and community in a Christ-centered atmosphere. To help make this happen, the facilitator encourages active listening and honest sharing. This person allows the material to facilitate opportunities for self-awareness and interaction with others.

Leadership is shared in a healthy group, but the facilitator is the one designated to set the pace, keep the group focused, and enable the members to support and care for each other.

People need to sense trust and freedom as the group develops; therefore, avoid "shoulds" or "musts" in your group.

3. Taking on a group ministry task can help members of your group balance personal growth with service to others.

In your first session, identify ways your group can offer help to others within the congregation or in your surrounding community. Take time at each meeting to do or arrange for that ministry task. Many times it is in the doing that we discover what we believe or how God is working in our lives.

4. Starting or continuing a personal action plan offers a way to address personal needs that you become aware of in your small-group experience.

For example, you might want to spend more time in conversation with a friend or spouse. Your action plan might state, "I plan to visit with Terry two times before our next small-group meeting."

If you decide to pursue a personal action plan, consider sharing it with your small group. Your group can be helpful in at least three ways: by giving support; helping to define the plan in realistic, measurable ways; and offering a source to whom you can be accountable.

5. Prayer is part of small-group fellowship. There is great power in group prayer, but not everyone feels free to offer spontaneous prayer. That's okay.

Learning to pray aloud takes time and practice. If you feel uncomfortable, start with simple and short prayers. And remember to pray for other members between sessions.

Use page 51 in the back of this book to note prayer requests made by group members.

6. Consider using a journal to help reflect on your experiences and insights between meeting times.

Writing about feelings, ideas, and questions can be one way to express yourself; plus it helps you remember what so often gets lost with time.

The "Daily Walk" component includes material that can get your journaling started. This, of course, is up to you and need not be done on any regular schedule. Even doing it once a week can be time well spent.

How to use this book

The material provided for each session is organized around some key components. If you are the facilitator for your small group, be sure to read this section carefully.

The facilitator's role is to establish a hospitable atmosphere and set a tone that encourages participants to share, reflect, and listen to each other. Some important practical things can help make this happen.

■ Whenever possible meet in homes. Be sure to provide clear directions about how to get there.

■ Use name tags for several sessions.

■ Place the chairs in a circle and close enough for everyone to hear and feel connected.

■ Be sure everyone has access to a book; preparation will pay off.

■ Have Bibles available and encourage participants to bring their own.

Welcoming

In this study, parents and guardians of young children can come together to explore how to nurture faith in their family and the lives of their children. This study provides a balance between understanding the faith of young children and developing practical ideas and strategies to nurture faith at home. Encourage the participants to put the ideas they explore into practice at home during the week. Parents and guardians of young children need encouragement and support in their efforts to build a family of faith!

Make necessary arrangements so that the physical and emotional environment for this group is as relaxed and comfortable as possible. Encourage people to come as they are, whether in business suits or gardening clothes. Make arrangements for child-care options to be available. Seek volunteer caregivers or shared child-care opportunities so that financial constraints do not keep people from attending.

Create a cozy atmosphere. Comfortable seating and space where everyone can converse with one another and be part of the group is vital. Encourage people to bring photos of their children to share with the group.

Focus

Each of the six chapter themes in this book has a brief focus statement. Read it aloud. It will give everyone a sense of the direction for each session and provide some boundaries so that people will not feel lost or frustrated trying to cover everything. The focus also connects the theme to the course topic.

Community building

This opening activity is crucial to a relaxed, friendly atmosphere. It will prepare the ground for gradual group development. Two "Community Building" options are provided under each theme. With the facilitator giving his or her response to the questions first, others are free to follow.

One purpose for this section is to allow everyone to participate as he or she responds to nonthreatening questions. The activity serves as a check-in time when participants are invited to share how things are going or what is new.

Make this time light and fun; remember, humor is a welcome gift. Use 15 to 20 minutes for this activity in your first few sessions and keep the entire group together.

During your first meeting, encourage group members to write down names and phone numbers (when appropriate) of the other members, so people can keep in touch. Use page 50 for this purpose.

Discovery

This component focuses on exploring the theme for your time together, using material that is read and questions and exercises that encourage sharing of personal insights and experiences.

Reading material includes a Bible text with supplemental passages and commentary written by the topic writer. Have volunteers read the Bible texts aloud. The main passage to be used is printed so that everyone operates from a common translation and sees the text.

"A Further Look" is included in some places to give you additional study material if time permits. Use it to explore related passages and questions. Be sure to have extra Bibles handy.

Questions and exercises related to the theme will invite personal sharing and storytelling. Keep in mind that as you listen to each other's stories, you are inspired to live more fully in the grace and will of God. Such exchanges make Christianity relevant and transformation more likely to happen. Caring relationships are key to clarifying one's beliefs. Sharing personal experiences and insights is what makes the small group spiritually satisfying.

Most people are open to sharing their life stories, especially if they're given permission to do so and they know someone will actively listen. Starting with the facilitator's response usually works best. On some occasions you may want to break the group into units of three or four persons to explore certain questions. When you reconvene, relate your experience to the whole group. Appoint someone to start the discussion.

Wrap-up

Plan your schedule so that there will be enough time for wrapping up. This time can include work on your group ministry task, review of key discoveries during your time together, identifying personal and prayer concerns, closing prayers, and the Lord's Prayer.

The facilitator can help the group identify and plan its ministry task. Introduce the idea and decide on your group ministry task in the first session. Tasks need not be grandiose. Activities might include:

- Ministry in your community, such as adopting a food shelf, clothes closet, or homeless shelter; sponsoring equipment, food, or clothing drives; or sending members to staff the shelter.

- Ministry to members of the congregation, such as writing notes to those who are ill or bereaved.

- Congregational tasks where volunteers are always needed, such as serving refreshments during the fellowship time after worship, stuffing envelopes for a church mailing, or taking responsibility for altar preparations for one month.

Depending upon the task, you can use part of each meeting time to carry out or plan the task.

In the "Wrap-up," allow time for people to share insights and encouragement and to voice special prayer requests. Just to mention someone who needs prayer is a form of prayer. The "Wrap-up" time may include a brief worship experience with candles, prayers, and singing. You might form a circle and hold hands. Silence can be effective. If you use the Lord's Prayer in your group, select the version that is known in your setting. There is space on page 50 to record the version your group uses. Another closing prayer is also printed on page 50. Before you go, ask members to pray for one another during the week. Remember also any special concerns or prayer requests.

Daily walk

Seven Bible readings and a verse, thought, and prayer for the journey related to the material just discussed are provided for those who want to keep the theme before them between sessions. These brief readings may be used for devotional time. Some group members may want to memorize selected passages. The Bible readings also can be used for supplemental study by the group if needed. Prayer for other group members also can be part of this time of personal reflection.

A word of encouragement

No material is ever complete or perfect for every situation or group. Creativity and imagination will be important gifts for the facilitator to bring to each theme. Keep in mind that it is in community that we are challenged to grow in Jesus Christ. Together we become what we could not become alone. It is God's plan that it be so.

For additional resources and ideas see *Starting Small Groups—and Keeping Them Going* (Minneapolis: Augsburg Fortress, 1995).

1 Nurturing the Faith of Preschoolers

Focus

We believe that God is already present in our home, in our children, and in ourselves! Our challenge is to discover God's gracious activity in our lives at home, and respond to it as a family with young children.

Community building

Option

As you look back on life when you were your child's age, how is life today most different and most similar? How do our children's ages (and our ages as parents) influence the way we live our lives as families?

Introduce yourselves to one another. Share your children's names and their ages. Then share your responses to these four unfinished sentences with each other.

- One of the best things about being a parent of a young child is . . .

- One of the most challenging things about being a parent of a young child is . . .

- One thing I've learned from my child is . . .

- One thing I still need to learn as a parent of a young child is . . .

Read the prayer together.

Opening prayer

Loving God, we give you thanks for our children—for their faith and joy, their sense of wonder and adventure. Open our eyes to the marvelous potential in our children and help us to see you at work in their lives each day. Amen

The journey of faith

Read aloud and then complete the statements.

Our lives as people of faith can be understood as a journey. In young childhood the gift of faith comes to us when we observe and imitate others, when we explore and test. It comes through feelings or sensory experiences we have at home or in church. The foundations of faith are laid when we learn to trust other people, ourselves, and our world, not because we are told to, but because we experience all of these as trustworthy. This means that our actions with our children influence their perceptions and their faith much more than what we say. Our children's faith life is shaped by how we treat them and what experiences we provide for them.

- As a child, faith for me was . . .
- As I grew, my understanding of faith changed. Now I see faith as . . .
- I want to pass on Christian faith to my child because . . .

The faith of young children

Read and reflect on these thoughts about nurturing the faith of young children. Then discuss the questions.

Faith growth in childhood involves many central needs: for approval and support, for a sense of belonging and assurance, for involvement in family life, and for exposure to a broader world. A child's faith life can be nurtured in a variety of ways that meet those needs. A key to faith growth is to develop a child's imagination and provide an order and routine that the child can trust.

To grow in faith, children need to experience God as a gracious parent and creator of all the good gifts they have. They can be encouraged to find God in the wonders around them, and to realize that God is part of all life. Although children may not find the words to describe their idea of God, God will speak and be revealed to them in ways they can understand.

Growth in faith is also nurtured when children develop an attitude of belonging to a church family, with its rituals, symbols, and stories. This happens when children experience church as the place where they find friends, loving acceptance, and happiness; where they can celebrate God's love and care in prayer and ritual.

Children need us to talk about Jesus in very human terms, emphasizing his goodness and kindness. When telling Bible stories or speaking about Jesus:

a. emphasize Jesus' caring and love for others.

b. make his life real for them by showing them they can be kind, loving, and helpful, like he was.

c. imaginatively retell favorite Bible stories to children in language appropriate for them, using situations they may have experienced and will understand.

Our challenge is to develop children's sense of awe and wonder and instill in them a sense of thanksgiving and community as we introduce them to God, our creator, and to Jesus, our Lord.

■ How do you see faith reflected in the life of your child?

■ What are some of the things you do or would like to do to nurture the faith of your young child?

Consider this

Search Institute has identified 40 developmental assets for children 3-5 years old. These assets help children start out well and grow up to be healthy, well adjusted, and strong. The 40 assets are grouped into eight categories: Support, Empowerment, Boundaries and Expectations, Constructive Use of Time, Commitment to Learning, Positive Values, Social Competencies, Positive Identity.

Throughout this book, we will connect children's spiritual growth with their overall growth using the Search assets.

To explore the importance of the assets for family life, look at the following assets: 1, 2, 7, 8, 14, 16, 19, 24, 25, 38, and 39. (See pages 52-53 for a list of the assets.) Then discuss the following questions.

■ How important are these assets for nurturing the faith growth of your child?

■ How can you strengthen your practice of these assets?

Group goals and ministry task

Read about group goals and group ministry tasks on pages 6-7 in this book. In groups of three, talk about the following questions. Then come back together.

- What do you hope to accomplish in this small-group course?

- Brainstorm group ministry task ideas that include the children of group members.

Bring your ideas to the whole group for discussion and decision making. Reaching out in Christ's love is a powerful way to learn. Consider projects aimed at the needs of young children, such as collecting food, toys, and clothing for parents and children in a local shelter; establishing a reading program for young children at your local library or church; or providing assistance to a preschool program. Record your goals and group ministry task in the appendix on page 51.

Discovery

Psalm 139:1-4

Read this Scripture passage aloud.

1 O Lord, you have searched me and known me.
2 You know when I sit down and when I rise up; you discern my thoughts from far away.
3 You search out my path and my lying down, and are acquainted with all my ways.
4 Even before a word is on my tongue, O Lord, you know it completely.

An atmosphere of faith

Read aloud and reflect on how to create an atmosphere of faith at home. Share responses with the group.

The faith of children is most easily nurtured in an atmosphere of faith. How do we create an atmosphere of faith in our homes and families? Here are a few ideas:

Value our children's experiences. When we help children reflect on simple life experiences, we put them in touch with faith stories. Whether it's their first encounter with ocean waves, a conflict over sharing toys, or learning to tell the truth, we reinforce the belief that God is active in their lives.

Introduce the wisdom of the community. Keeping in mind children's simple life experiences, we share stories from the life of Jesus and the church that pertain to their faith story.

Create an atmosphere of dialogue. Here we attempt to relate the story of our children with the story of our faith. We want them to see that the God of our faith, who has been at work throughout history, is at work in their lives and in their story.

Gently challenge toward response. We ask a few questions and make a few suggestions to help our children live their faith. We cannot force a response, but try to encourage and support genuine responses to God.

- How do you try to create an atmosphere of faith at home with your preschooler?

- How would you use the four suggestions in your family? Think of practical ways you can use these ideas.

Discovery

Read and discuss.

Growing in faith together

As parents, we need to create the atmosphere for our children to discover God's presence and respond to it. But we can only give them what we really experience in our own lives. This means we need to be open to God's gift of faith and spiritual growth ourselves!

For faith to be lived and real it must connect with life experiences. We can take advantage of teachable moments that occur each day in the bathtub, at the dinner table, and even in front of the TV. When we recognize God's activity in our children, we can point it out to them. However, if we are unaware of God's presence in our own lives, we will have difficulty seeing God in theirs. An artist has a good eye and a strong intuitive sense of what lies beneath the surface of the canvas. Like artists, we can reveal the beauty of God's love that often lies just beneath the surface.

To learn more about parenting young children and to find a variety of family activities and ideas, see the resource list on page 54.

The Bible stories we share, the rituals we celebrate, the ways we pray together, and the ways we serve other people must be connected to lives rooted in faith if they are to bear fruit. To the extent that our faith is lived and real, it will rub off on our children. When we are in touch with our own faith, our teaching and actions will come across with conviction, because there is genuine depth and richness to them and they are a natural part of our lives. When we allow ourselves to grow in faith, we help our children to see that spiritual growth can continue throughout life. We can live and grow in faith together in our families.

- What do you do—or what would you like to do—to develop an atmosphere for faith in your own life?

- In the last month, have you seen God at work in your life? In your child's life? What might help you to be more aware of God's presence in daily life?

Have copies of recent worship bulletins or church newsletters available.

- What does your congregation offer that might give you the opportunity to grow in faith? What does it offer that might give you and your children the opportunity to grow in faith together?

A further look

Read the passage and then take time, individually, to write responses. Share insights with the group.

A parent's baptismal promise

At Baptism, parents promise to train their children in the practice of the Christian faith, to bring up their children to keep God's commandments as Christ taught us, by loving God and neighbor. Think about how you live your baptismal promise with your children today. As you reflect on what you discovered in this session, consider new ways you can live your baptismal promise starting tomorrow.

- Ways I currently live my baptismal promise . . .

- New ways I can live my baptismal responsibility . . .

Wrap-up

See pages 9 in the introduction for a description of "Wrap-up."

Before you go, take time for the following:

- Group ministry task

- Review

See page 50 for suggested closing prayers. Page 51 can also be used for listing ongoing prayer requests.

- Personal concerns and prayer concerns

- Closing prayers

Daily walk

Bible readings

Day 1
John 15:1-11

Day 2
John 15:12-17

Day 3
Romans 12:9-18

Day 4
1 Corinthians 13:1-8

Day 5
1 John 4:7-21

Day 6
Psalm 136

Day 7
Psalm 145

Verse for the journey

But you are a chosen race, a royal priesthood, a holy nation, God's own people, in order that you may proclaim the mighty acts of him who called you out of darkness into his marvelous light. 1 Peter 2:9

Thought for the journey

Once upon a time, the story goes, a preacher ran through the streets of the city shouting, "We must put God into our lives. We must put God into our lives." And hearing him, an old monk rose up in the city plaza to say, "No, sir, you are wrong. You see, God is already in our lives. Our task is simply to recognize that."

Prayer for the journey

God, give us the power to love. Help us to put love at the center of our family's life and make it the focus of our energies. May we grow more in love with you each day. Amen

2 Sharing Faith and Values

Through love and devoted commitment, parents teach young children the essential values of the Christian life— values that will become children's building blocks for living as followers of Jesus their entire lives.

Community building

Have writing paper and pens or pencils available.

In this chapter, we will reflect on the values or "instructions for living" we want to share with our children and look at how to do this.

Values worth sharing

Take time to reflect on your values and write them down, then share your responses with the group.

Values I learned at home: Identify several important values you learned at home when you were growing up.

Values we share: Identify the values you want to share with your child. Place a check mark next to the values you feel are real strengths in your family.

Option

Imagine that you are moving and can take only five of your most important possessions. (The people in your family and your pets are already safely moved.) What specifically would you take? Why would you choose these things? What does this say about the values you hold?

Opening prayer

Listen, my people, mark each word. I begin with a story, I speak of mysteries welling up from ancient depths. We must not hide this story from our children but tell the mighty works and all the wonders of God.

Psalm 78:1-4, adapted

The values of Jesus

Discuss the questions. Have a number of children's Bibles and storybooks available for learning about Jesus.

- ◼ If your child asked you who Jesus is, what would you say? What images, stories, and examples would you use to talk about Jesus?

- ◼ How does your answer to your child reflect who Jesus is for you today?

Our children need to know Jesus and to learn how to live as he lived. What should we say about Jesus? You might find children's Bibles or storybooks helpful in sharing the following insights and stories with your child.

God sent Jesus to us as a baby in Bethlehem (Jesus' birth and childhood: Matthew 1–2, Luke 1–2).

Jesus brings good news to us (Jesus' mission: Luke 4:16-21, Luke 7:18-23).

Jesus asks us to follow him (calling the disciples: Matthew 4:18-22, Mark 1:16-20, Luke 5:1-11, John 1:35-51; Mary Magdalene follows Jesus: Luke 8:1-3, Matthew 27:55-61 and 28:1-10, John 20:11-18).

Jesus wants us to live in peace, love, and forgiveness (the good Samaritan: Luke 10:25-37; the final judgment: Matthew 25:31-40).

Jesus loves us and cares about all people (Jesus choosing Matthew the tax collector: Matthew 9:9-13; the man with paralysis: Luke 5:17-26; Jairus' daughter: Luke 8:40-42 and 49-56; the ten lepers: Luke 17:11-19; the man who was blind: Luke 18:35-43, the widow's son: Luke 7:11-17; blessing the children: Matthew 19:13-15; the lost sheep: Matthew 18:10-14, Luke 15:1-7; the great banquet: Luke 14:15-24).

Jesus teaches us to pray (the Lord's Prayer: Luke 11:1-13, Matthew 6:5-15 and 7:7-11; times when Jesus prayed: Mark 1:32-39, Luke 5:15-16, Luke 6:12-13; Luke 22:39-46; John 17).

Jesus is alive today (Jesus rises on Easter: Mark 16, Matthew 28, Luke 24).

- ◼ What insights did you gain from this list? How might you strengthen your response to your child's question about Jesus?

Matthew 7:24-27

Have a person read the Gospel passage aloud to the group.

24 Everyone then who hears these words of mine and acts on them will be like a wise man who built his house on rock. 25 The rain fell, the floods came, and the winds blew and beat on that house, but it did not fall, because it had been founded on rock. 26 And everyone who hears these words of mine and does not act on them will be like a foolish man who built his house on sand. 27 The rain fell, and the floods came, and the winds blew and beat against that house, and it fell—and great was its fall!

Values for living

Jesus' teachings address the vision, values, and actions that characterize the life of a disciple. Learn more about Gospel values by reading the following passages.

Give each person a Bible. Assign one or more values to each person or to teams. Ask the participants to read the Scripture passages and identify the Gospel's particular understanding of this value. After several minutes, ask each person or team to share insights.

1. Love: Luke 10:25-37 and 6:27-36
2. Care and compassion: Luke 7:1-16 and 8:40-55
3. Generosity and hospitality: Matthew 15:32-39, Luke 14:15-23
4. Forgiveness: Matthew 5:21-26 and 18:21-35
5. Peace: Matthew 5:9, 21-24, 38-48
6. Faithfulness: Luke 1:26-37 and 24:1-9
7. Humility and integrity: Luke 18:9-14 and 6:47-49
8. Courage and endurance: Luke 18:1-8, John 18:33-38 and 19:1-11
9. Respect for human dignity: Luke 7:36-50 and 13:10-17
10. Service: John 13:1-17 and Matthew 25:31-46
11. Justice: Luke 16:19-31 and 19:1-10

Apply these Gospel values to life today by discussing these questions.

- What are some of the challenges of living the wisdom of Jesus in our families and in the world today?

- What would have to change in your life in order to live the message of Jesus more fully?

- How can you find the support and strength to meet the challenge of discipleship today?

Consider this

Review the six positive values, assets 26-31, and then discuss the questions.

Search Institute has identified six positive values that are essential for healthy growth: caring, equality and social justice, integrity, honesty, responsibility, and healthy lifestyle. Turn to pages 52-53 to read the descriptions of each value in assets 26-31.

- Why are these values so important for healthy, positive growth?

- How do these values connect with Gospel values?

Sharing values at home

Ask one person to read the passage from Proverbs aloud and then discuss the questions.

"Train children in the right way, and when old, they will not stray" (Proverbs 22:6).

■ What are several ways you share and live Gospel values at home with your child?

■ What are some of the obstacles that hinder your efforts to teach values to your child?

Review the 10 ingredients and then discuss the questions.

From *501 Practical Ways to Teach Your Children Values* by Bobbie Reed © 1998 Concordia Publishing House. Used with permission.

In the book *501 Practical Ways to Teach Your Children Values* (pages 11-13), Bobbie Reed identifies 10 "ingredients" for sharing your value system with your child.

1. **Identify your own values.** Before you can teach your children, you need to be clear about what you want them to learn. . . .

2. **Tell your children what your values are.** Learn to state clearly and concisely what you believe and how these values influence decisions in your life. . . .

3. **Explain the values.** . . . Describe to your children the behaviors that demonstrate those qualities. . . .

4. **Explore the values.** Help your children understand values by using a variety of teaching methods, and inviting discussions about values. . . .

5. **Model what you want your children to say and do.** . . . [Let your children] observe you as a living model of the values you teach. . . .

6. **Teach values with Bible stories.** Whenever you can teach a value by telling a Bible story, your children benefit twice. First, they learn more about values. Second, they also increase their knowledge and understanding of God's Word. . . .

7. **Apply values in everyday experiences.** The key to passing on values is to help children see how those values apply to daily life. Explain that choices reveal values. For example, a person who does a kind deed for a stranger demonstrates that kindness is one of his or her values.

8. **Reinforce values through games.** Your children learn a lot about life as they play. . . . Be creative and you will find many ways to make learning a game.

9. **Reward children when they live out Christian values**. . . . Positive reinforcement effectively shapes children's choices.

10. **Celebrate as a family.** When your children pass a major milestone in their acceptance of the values you are teaching, . . . celebrate! . . .

■ What did you find most helpful in this list of 10 ingredients?

■ What are several practical ways that you can apply these nine ingredients in your family?

Putting values into practice

Take time to review what you have learned and complete the Family Coat of Values.

Create a Family Coat of Values. Put your family name at the top. In each of the six sections write a value with one or two ways you want your family to live out this value.

Family Coat of Values

Identify one value and how you want to live out this value. Share your ideas with the group.

When you get home, hold a brief family meeting to share your values and ideas with your child and invite him or her to add ideas. As a family, commit to living these six values over the next several months. Post your plan on the refrigerator (or other prominent place in the house). Review your success at the end of each month.

To learn more about parenting young children and to find a variety of family activities and ideas, see the resource list on page 54.

Consider this

Take one Gospel value and develop a plan for living that value in your home for one month. Post your plan on the refrigerator (or other prominent place in the house). Review your success at the end of the month and identify a value for the new month. Keep a record of your monthly values and action plans.

A further look

Read aloud the reflection on Baptism, then share ideas for a symbol or image.

In Baptism we promise to guide our children in putting on the mind and heart of Christ. As Paul says, "Let the same mind be in you that was in Christ Jesus" (Philippians 2:5). When we adopt and live the values of Jesus we are putting on the mind and heart of Christ.

■ Think of a symbol or image for your family that reflects putting on the mind and heart of Christ.

■ Take time at home to create or find this symbol and display it in a special place to remind everyone of living the values of Jesus.

Wrap-up

Before you go, take time for the following:

- Group ministry task

- Review

- Personal concerns and prayer concerns

- Closing prayers

Daily walk

Bible readings

Day 1
Matthew 5:1-12

Day 2
Matthew 5:21-26

Day 3
Matthew 5:38-42

Day 4
Matthew 5:43-48

Day 5
Matthew 7:1-5

Day 6
Matthew 25:31-46

Day 7
Matthew 22:34-40

Verse for the journey

For where your treasure is, there your heart will be also.
Matthew 6:21.

Thought for the journey

When we adopt and live the values of Jesus we are putting on the mind and heart of Christ.

Prayer for the journey

Lord God, help us to put on the mind and heart of Jesus. Teach us and our children to live out gospel values. Amen

3 Celebrating Rituals as a Family

Focus

It would be helpful to have a number of family ritual books available to review during the session. See the resource list on page 54 for suggestions.

Rituals are essential for our family life. Family rituals give us a sense of permanence, the assurance that even the most ordinary of family activities are meaningful and significant.

Community building

Reflect on the questions and share stories with the group.

In this chapter, we will have an opportunity to explore the importance of family rituals and create a family calendar of ritual celebrations to observe through the year. We begin by taking time to recall a religious ritual your family celebrated when you were growing up: rituals for daily life (prayer before meals, prayer at night), seasons of the church year (Christmas, Lent, Easter), seasonal celebrations (Thanksgiving), family milestones or life transitions (birth/baptism, birthday, anniversary, death/funeral), or ethnic rituals and traditions.

Option

Recall one experience of worship or ritual celebration that really moved you. How did this affect you? Why was this experience meaningful to you? Did you experience God through this worship service or ritual?

- Recall one significant ritual or celebration that your family observed together when you were growing up.

- Was this ritual meaningful to you?

- Did you experience God through this ritual?

Opening prayer

1 Make a joyful noise to the LORD, all the earth.
2   Worship the LORD with gladness;
    come into his presence with singing.
3 Know that the LORD is God.
    It is he that made us, and we are his;
    we are his people, and the sheep of his pasture.

Psalm 100

The importance of family ritual

Family rituals can be extremely simple or more involved. Some rituals occur daily—in the morning, before and after meals, or at bedtime—while others come along weekly, yearly, or once in a lifetime. They can be used to observe special days, such as Christmas and birthdays, as well as the more routine times in family life. Rituals are appropriate during times of celebration as well as loss.

When we observe rituals that have been handed down through the years or create new ones just for our families, we help our children to live and grow in faith. Rituals provide opportunities for children and parents to slow down and see God's presence in each day, think about the meaning of life's major events and daily happenings, and celebrate God's goodness.

- What role do rituals of faith play in your life today? In your family's life?

- What role would you like rituals of faith to play in your family's life?

Ecclesiastes 3:1-2, 4, 6-7

1 For everything there is a season, and a time for every matter under heaven:
2   a time to be born, and a time to die;
**   a time to plant, and a time to pluck up what is**
**   planted; . . .**
4   a time to weep, and a time to laugh;
**   a time to mourn, and a time to dance; . . .**
6   a time to seek, and a time to lose;
**   a time to keep, and a time to throw away;**
7   a time to tear, and a time to sew;
**   a time to keep silence, and a time to speak.**

Daily rituals

Rituals throughout the day help us to recognize and celebrate God's everyday presence in our family life. Think about the many opportunities in your daily family life for celebrating a ritual of faith: prayer in the morning; table blessings (before and after meals); telling and reading Bible stories; leaving for school or work; times of thanksgiving, joy or sorrow; times for forgiveness and healing; and bedtime prayers, stories, and blessings.

■ What are the possibilities for daily rituals of faith in your family today?

A further look

Complete the daily rituals plan, then share your ideas with the group.

Developing a daily rituals plan

Rituals are so important for nurturing family faith growth. Your family's traditions and rituals can begin now, or you can continue or revise rituals passed down in your family.

Identify rituals that are already a part of your family life and new rituals that you would like to incorporate into your week. Use the following chart as a guide for planning.

Daily Rituals Plan

Sunday	
Monday	
Tuesday	
Wednesday	
Thursday	
Friday	
Saturday	

Seasons of the church year

Read about seasons of the church year and life transitions, and discuss the questions.

The possibilities for celebrating the seasons of the church year at home are numerous. For example, in one family's ritual for Ash Wednesday, each family member draws a symbol of a personal weakness that he or she intends to work on during Lent. This may range from vowing to make the bed each day, to putting on a happy face, to helping someone. These symbols are shared, placed in a foil-lined dish, and burned as an offering to the Lord. Afterward, the ashes are placed in a small jar on the dinner table where everyone can see them, as a gentle reminder of the Lenten promises.

Each season offers opportunities for celebrating rituals and offering prayers at home.

- What are the possibilities for celebrating the seasons of the church year in your family today?

Life transitions and milestones

There are regular opportunities in family life for celebrating life transitions and milestones. For example, one family had an impromptu blessing of their children's bikes on the day the youngest finally learned how to ride, celebrating the wonderful freedom and independence of "having wheels." Think about the possibilities in your family to observe births or adoptions and baptisms, birthdays, wedding anniversaries, Mother's Day and Father's Day, learning how to walk, starting school or preschool, a new job, moving to a new home, and deaths or funerals.

- What are the possibilities for celebrating life transitions and milestones in your family today?

A further look

Complete the Yearly Rituals Plan, then share ideas with the group. Review the books and resources as you complete the plan.

Developing a yearly rituals plan

Think about the many opportunities for celebrating rituals of faith throughout the year: seasons of the church, calendar seasons, and family transitions/milestones. Identify rituals that are already a part of your family life and new rituals that you would like to incorporate into your year. Use the chart on page 28 as a guide for planning your year. Add the dates for family milestones.

	Church season Calendar seasons Life transitions	Family Ritual Activity
December	Advent Christmas	
January	Epiphany Martin Luther King Jr.'s birthday	
February	Valentine's Day Ash Wednesday	
March	Lent	
April	Holy Week Easter	
May	Pentecost Mother's Day	
June	Father's Day	
July		
August	Start of school	
September		
October	Reformation Day	
November	All Saints Day	

Consider displaying your completed ritual plan on the refrigerator (or other prominent place in the house). Review your success at the end of the month or season and identify a ritual for the new month or season. Keep a record of your monthly rituals and action plans.

Consider this

The Search Institute has found that children can develop a positive identity when families have a sense of purpose and demonstrate a positive view of the future. Read the descriptions of assets 39 and 40 on page 53.

■ **How can these assets connect with your family's rituals?**

Begin a family scrapbook of rituals using drawings, snapshots, explanations, poems, reflections. Individual family members can add to the book by sharing their feelings about the event or simply recording the who, what, where, why, when of the event. This is a great way to pass on rituals to the next generation. It is also fun to see and read about your rituals as time turns them into memories.

A further look

Set up a prayer table with a large white candle, Bible, bowl of water, and small bowl of olive oil. Light the candle as you begin. Play instrumental music in the background.

Recalling the baptismal celebration

In this chapter, we will remember baptism through a prayer service.

■ Gather prayerfully around the table.

■ Have someone read about Jesus' baptism from Mark 1:9-11.

■ Pass the bowl of water around the group. One-by-one, dip your hand in the water and make the sign of the cross on your forehead. As each person does this, everyone prays: "May these waters renew the grace of your baptism in you."

■ Pass the bowl of olive oil around the group. One-by-one, dip your hand in the oil and make the sign of the cross on your forehead. As each does this, everyone prays: "May Christ strengthen you with his love and power."

■ Close this prayer service by reading Psalm 23.

Wrap-up

Before you go, take time for the following:

■ Group ministry task

■ Review

■ Personal concerns and prayer concerns

■ Closing prayers

Daily walk

Bible readings

Day 1
Luke 22:7-20

Day 2
Acts 2:37-42

Day 3
Psalm 95:1-7

Day 4
Acts 2:43-47

Day 5
Psalm 63:1-8

Day 6
Mark 1:9-11

Day 7
Micah 6:6-8

Verse for the journey

O come, let us worship and bow down, let us kneel before the LORD, our Maker! Psalm 95:6

Thought for the journey

To be effective and joyful parents, we must learn to celebrate all of family life, both the extraordinary—special days like birthdays, feast days and holidays—and the ordinary, finding God in our mealtimes, bedtimes, playtimes, work times. We do this by creating ritual moments.

From *The Art of Tradition* by and © 1998 Mary Caswell Walsh. Used by permission.

Prayer for the journey

Lord, guide us as we celebrate the seasons of faith in our family. Draw us closer together as we celebrate your presence throughout our day and throughout our year. Amen

4 Praying as a Family

Focus

It would be helpful to have a number of prayer resources for families with young children available to review during the session. See the resource list on page 54 for suggestions.

Prayer is the very heart of our encounter and relationship with God. If prayer constitutes the soul of the Christian spiritual life, prayer also must lie at the center of family spirituality.

Community building

Reflect and discuss.

Prayer in the family begins with us as parents. This chapter explores the role of prayer in your life and the life of your family and looks at ways to strengthen your family's prayer life.

- Do you pray? Is prayer part of your everyday life?

- If you pray, what do you pray *for* or pray *about*?

- Can you think of a prayer time when you felt close to God?

Option

Describe your prayer life today using a color, a song or hymn, a weather condition, and a part of nature (sunset, mountains, ocean).

Read the psalm together.

Opening prayer

1 It is good to give thanks to the LORD,
   to sing praises to your name, O Most High;
2 to declare your steadfast love in the morning,
   and your faithfulness by night,
3 to the music of the lute and the harp,
   to the melody of the lyre.
4 For you, O LORD, have made me glad by your work;
   at the works of your hands I sing for joy.

Psalm 92:1-4

Romans 8:26-27

Read the Scripture passage together.

26 The Spirit helps us in our weakness; for we do not know how to pray as we ought, but that very Spirit intercedes with sighs too deep for words. 27 And God, who searches the heart, knows what is the mind of the Spirit, because the Spirit intercedes for the saints according to the will of God.

Exploring prayer

Discuss the questions, read the reflection on prayer, then discuss the question that follows the reflection.

■ How do you define *prayer*?

■ What does prayer mean to you?

God is always present and active in our lives. We can respond to God's gracious presence with prayers of joy, thanksgiving, and petition, with the assurance that God's Spirit works for the good of all.

When we teach children to pray, first we need to help them identify God's presence in their daily lives. Because children often have relationships with someone or something that is real to them but unseen, prayer can be easier for them than adults. With our help, they can find helpful images of God in Scripture, the Christian tradition, and their own experience.

■ Why would regular prayer be important for your life and your family's life?

Five forms of prayer

This would be a good time to display prayer resources. Give examples of each of the five forms of prayer.

You and your child can learn to use these five forms of prayer:

Prayers of praise: We give praise to God for being good, for the mystery and majesty of God.

Prayers of thanksgiving: We give thanks to God for the many gifts God shares with us, for all that we have and are. We can also thank God for what we need even before we have it, trusting that God will provide for our needs.

Spontaneous prayers: There are times when we need to say what is in our heart and, with the Spirit's leading, let prayer flow spontaneously out of our deepest selves.

Prayers of petition: We ask God for what we need as well as what others need. We offer these prayers because they remind us that we need God above all.

Prayers of contrition: We acknowledge that we are imperfect, that we make mistakes and sometimes choose wrong behavior that affects us and our relationship to God and to others.

- Are you familiar with any of these five prayer forms? If so, which ones?

- How can you use these five forms of prayer in your family?

Prayer is a discipline that takes practice. Identify times during the day or week that you can more fully incorporate prayer into your family life, such as mealtime and bedtime. Set a time each day when you can spend 15-20 minutes in prayer.

A further look

If time allows, have each person read one Bible passage silently and share her or his findings with the group.

The stories in the Bible show us how people turn to God in every situation of their lives, knowing that God is listening and ready to respond.

Take a few minutes to explore these stories of people praying in the Bible.

  a. Genesis 18:16-33
  b. 1 Samuel 1:9-18
  c. 1 Kings 3:3-14
  d. 2 Kings 19:14-20
  e. Psalm 51:10-12
  f. Psalm 63:1-7
  g. Matthew 15:21-28
  h. Luke 1:46-55
  i. Luke 1:67-79
  j. Acts 7:59-60
  k. Acts 16:25-36
  l. 1 Timothy 2:1-2

Guiding children in prayer

Read and discuss.

■ What can you do to help your child learn to pray?

How can you guide your child in prayer? Here are several suggestions from the book *Children and Prayer* by Betty Shannon Cloyd, adapted from chapter 5:

Adapted from *Children and Prayer: A Shared Pilgrimage.* © 1997 Betty Shannon Cloyd. Used by permission of Upper Room Books.

a. Pray as you can in the midst of your busy day.
b. Use your child's name in prayer so she knows she is important to you and to God.
c. Establish patterns of prayer in your family life that encourage your child to pray.
d. Help your child to pray by watching you pray and imitating you.
e. Repeat familiar prayers to nurture security in your child.
f. Teach your child to use his own words in prayer.
g. Encourage your child to pray any time, anywhere, under any circumstance, and to say anything to God she wants to say.
h. Guide your child to use formal and spontaneous prayers, prayers of praise and thanksgiving, prayers for himself and others, and prayers asking for forgiveness.

■ Which suggestions do you find most helpful? How might you begin to use these ideas in your family?

Building up assets

While learning to pray is essential for children's spiritual growth, it can also build up the assets necessary for overall growth and well-being. Take a look at the Search Institute assets and their definitions on pages 52-53 (especially 20, 26, 27, 33, 37, 39, and 40).

■ Which of the assets could be reinforced during individual and family times of prayer?

■ Which of these assets would you like to build up during times of prayer with your child?

Review these ideas for home activities.

Consider this

Family altar

Create a family altar for prayer and ritual. Find a place in your home (kitchen, family room) that you can set aside and decorate as your family altar or prayer space. Include a Bible, candles, art, photographs, and prayer books on your altar.

Family prayer scrapbook

Begin a family book of prayers using drawings, snapshots, explanations, poems, and reflections.

Prayer journals

Help your child create a prayer journal. Journal entries can include letters to God, prayers of the heart, artwork, and so forth. Once a month, invite the family to gather for prayer, inviting members to share from their prayer journals.

A further look

Baptism connection

Baptism immerses us into a life with God who is Three in One: God our parent and provider; Jesus our redeemer and friend; the Holy Spirit our sanctifier and consolation. The Lord's Prayer connects us to this life, reminding us of who we are and what our Christian lives are all about.

Pray together the Lord's Prayer from Luke 11:1-4.

- What does the Lord's Prayer reveal to us about ourselves?

- What does the Lord's Prayer reveal to us about prayer and the Christian life?

Wrap-up

Before you go, take time for the following:

- Group ministry task

- Review

- Personal concerns and prayer concerns

- Closing prayers

Daily walk

Bible readings

Day 1
Psalm 148

Day 2
Psalm 116

Day 3
Psalm 95:1-7

Day 4
Psalm 71

Day 5
Psalm 20

Day 6
Psalm 111

Day 7
Psalm 143

Verse for the journey

Ask, and it will be given you; search, and you will find; knock, and the door will be opened for you. For everyone who asks receives, and everyone who searches finds, and for everyone who knocks, the door will be opened. Matthew 7:7-8.

Thought for the journey

Prayer is a discipline that takes practice.

Prayer for the journey

Lord, make us instruments of your peace.
　　Where there is hatred, let us sow love;
　　　where there is injury, pardon;
　　　where there is discord, union;
　　　where there is doubt, faith;
　　　where there is despair, hope;
　　　where there is darkness, light;
　　　where there is sadness, joy.

Adapted from "A Prayer Attributed to St. Francis," *LBW*, p. 48, copyright © 1978

5 Serving as a Family

If possible, make available several books about opportunities for children and families to serve. See the resource list on page 54 for suggestions. A list of service projects sponsored by your church or community would also be helpful.

Focus

The call to serve and work for justice is a central theme in the Bible. When families serve the needs of others, they follow in the footsteps of Jesus and grow in faith as a family.

Community building

Reflect and discuss.

- When you think of serving, *what* comes to mind?
- When you think of serving, *who* comes to mind?
- Why do you think it is important for Christians to serve others?

Option

Complete the following unfinished sentences.

- A social problem I wish we could fix is . . .

- The world would be a better place if . . .

- A person who embodies a life of justice and service is . . .

- In the past, I was involved in serving others when . . .

Opening prayer

Lord, teach us what it means to be poor in spirit in a consumer society; to comfort those who suffer in our midst; to show mercy in an often unforgiving world; to hunger and thirst for justice in a nation still challenged by hunger and homelessness, poverty and prejudice; and to be peacemakers in an often violent and fearful world. Amen

The least of these

Invite one person to read this section aloud. Then discuss the questions.

Our Christian faith calls us to work for justice; to serve those in need; to pursue peace; and to defend the life, dignity, and rights of all our sisters and brothers. This is the call of Jesus, the challenge of the prophets, and the living tradition of the church.

Matthew 25:34-40

34 Then the king will say to those at his right hand, "Come, you that are blessed by my Father, inherit the kingdom prepared for you from the foundation of the world; 35 for I was hungry and you gave me food, I was thirsty and you gave me something to drink, I was a stranger and you welcomed me, 36 I was naked and you gave me clothing, I was sick and you took care of me, I was in prison and you visited me." 37 Then the righteous will answer him, "Lord, when was it that we saw you hungry and gave you food, or thirsty and gave you something to drink? 38 And when was it that we saw you a stranger and welcomed you, or naked and gave you clothing? 39 And when was it that we saw you sick or in prison and visited you?" 40 And the king will answer them, "Truly I tell you, just as you did it to one of the least of these who are members of my family, you did it to me."

- ■ What does this passage say to you about the importance of justice and service in the Christian faith?

- ■ Jesus says, "just as you did it to one of the least of these who are members of my family, you did it to me." What does this mean for us?

Christ among us

Read and discuss.

From *Words to Love by . . .Mother Teresa* by Mother Teresa, compiled and edited by Frank Cunningham. © 1983 Ave Maria Press, PO Box 248, Notre Dame, IN 46556. Used with permission of the publisher.

In *Words to Love By . . .* (page 80), Mother Teresa explained why she spent her life serving the "least of these" in Calcutta:

> At the end of life we will not be judged by
>> how many diplomas we have received
>> how much money we have made
>> how many great things we have done.

> We will be judged by
>> "I was hungry and you gave me food to eat,
>> I was naked and you clothed me
>> I was homeless and you took me in."

Hungry not only for bread
      —but hungry for love
Naked not only for clothing
      —but naked of human dignity and respect
Homeless not only for want of a room of bricks
      —but homeless because of rejection.

This is Christ in distressing disguise.

■ Can you think of some people in need of food, clothing, or shelter?

■ Can you think of some people in need of love, respect, and acceptance?

■ How would you like your child or your family to respond to these needs—and to Christ?

Form groups of two or three and assign one Scripture passage to each group. Share responses to the questions with the large group.

Consider this

The Bible is rich in teachings on justice and service. Read your assigned Scripture passage and prepare a response to the following question: What does this passage teach us about the importance of justice and service in the Christian faith?

Leviticus 19:9-18	Luke 16:19-31
Isaiah 58:6-10	John 13:1-15
Luke 4:16-19	2 Corinthians 9:6-15
Luke 10:25-37	James 2:1-17

Imagine what the world would be like if the principles embodied in the Bible became a reality in our time. What would it mean for your life, your family's life, your community, and our nation and world?

Serving as a family

Have everyone read this section quietly, then discuss the questions.

The significance of Christ's love and justice in our lives is reflected in how we treat our spouses and children and how we spend our time and money. The lessons we teach our children through our words and actions influence their commitment to justice and caring for the "least among us."

Working together, parents and young children can become involved in the work of justice and service in so many ways. This involvement gives you opportunities to talk with your child about the importance of serving others and following Jesus. Think about doing these activities as a family:

a. Prepare and serve a meal at a soup kitchen or homeless shelter.

b. Donate food to a local food bank or donate toys and clothes for children in need.

c. Visit the elderly at a convalescent home or senior-citizen facility.

d. Do chores and shopping for the homebound.

e. Care for the environment by recycling and by planting trees or a garden in your community.

f. Give generously to those in need at home and abroad through financial donations to local and national groups that work directly with the poor or work for justice on behalf of the poor.

g. Pray regularly for greater justice and peace.

h. Learn more about the Bible's teaching on justice, peace, and service.

i. Advocate for public policies that protect life, promote human dignity, preserve God's creation, and build peace.

j. With other families, work for greater charity, justice, and peace.

k. Consider adopting a family service project each month or each season, especially during the Advent-Christmas and Lenten seasons.

■ How are individuals and families already involved in service projects in your church and community?

■ How is your church engaged in the work of justice and service?

■ What organizations in your community are engaged in the work of justice and service? Who do they serve?

■ How can your family become involved in justice and service—locally and globally?

The benefits of service

Review assets 9, 26, and 27, and the benefits of service. Then discuss the questions.

Three of the 40 assets for healthy development from the Search Institute explicitly focus on the importance of the service: service to others (9), family values caring (26), and family values equality and social justice (27). Read about these on pages 52-53.

The following key points have been made in the research and work of the Search Institute:

Serving helps make the Christian faith real: It provides hands-on experiences and opportunities for growth.

Serving promotes healthy lifestyles and choices: It develops values and priorities that help children make positive choices.

Serving helps develop positive self-esteem, self-confidence, and social skills: As people serve, they learn that they can make a difference in the world and that they have important things to contribute.

Serving helps people discover their personal gifts and abilities: Serving increases self-esteem and moral reasoning abilities.

Serving teaches new skills and perspectives: Families see the world with a new perspective when they've been exposed to different people and different needs.

Serving nurtures a lifelong commitment to service and justice: Children who learn to serve when they are young are more likely to be service oriented when they are adults.

Serving builds a stronger sense of community within the family and among families who serve: The experience of serving together can draw families closer.

Serving has an impact on people who are served: Their needs are met, and they receive a sense of hope and empowerment. Families can have an impact on critical issues facing the community, nation, and the world.

Serving improves the quality of life and the climate of the community: Serving not only meets important needs, it also gives people a sense that things can be done to make the community a better place.

- What do you see as the benefits of serving as a family? Which benefits seem most important or significant to you?

- How can serving benefit you and your child?

A further look

Read this section aloud. Then take time to complete the pledge and share ideas about it.

A family commitment to serve

Baptism empowers us for our mission as Christians. It has been said that no one can do everything, but everyone can do something. Each of us has unique abilities, a certain amount of time, and financial resources. Are there changes that you can make in allocating your talent, time, and treasure so  that you can more effectively serve those in need and promote the work of justice—locally, nationally, and globally?

Reaffirm your baptismal mission by creating a family pledge for justice and service.

A pledge

He has told you, O mortal, what is good;
and what does the Lord require of you but to do justice,
and to love kindness,
and to walk humbly with your God?

Micah 6:8

In an attempt to act justly and serve those in need, our family will . . .

_____

_____

_____

_____

_____

_____

_____

_____

Wrap-up

Before you go, take time for the following:

- Group ministry task

- Review

- Personal concerns and prayer concerns

- Closing prayers

Daily walk

Bible readings

Day 1
John 13:1-15

Day 2
Isaiah 2:1-5

Day 3
Isaiah 61:1-2

Day 4
Psalm 146

Day 5
Luke 3:10-18

Day 6
Acts 4:32-35

Day 7
1 John 4:19-21

Verse for the journey

He has told you, O mortal, what is good; and what does the Lord require of you but to do justice, and to love kindness, and to walk humbly with your God? Micah 6:8

Thought for the journey

The lessons we teach our children through our words and actions influence their commitment to justice and caring for the "least among us."

Prayer for the journey

God, true light and source of all light, may we recognize you in oppressed people and poor people, in homeless people and hungry people. May we be open to your Spirit that we may be a means of healing, strength, and peace for all your people. We ask this in the name of Jesus, your Son. Amen

6 Relating as a Family

Focus

It would be helpful to have a number of parenting and family enrichment books available to review during the session. See the resource list on page 54 for suggestions.

Effective parenting and a strong home life evolve from commitment—from a determination to build upon your family's strengths and upon the gift of faith in God.

Community building

Allow time for everyone to reflect on the questions, then invite responses. Keep the focus on sharing and storytelling.

- One of my greatest gifts or strengths as a parent of young children is . . .
- A story that illustrates one of my parenting gifts or strengths is . . .

Option

Describe your family life today using a TV commercial; a TV show, Broadway musical or feature film; a popular song; or a popular book title.

Opening prayer

Gracious God, give us the strength and wisdom to build families on the foundations of love and compassion, kindness and generosity, humility and gentleness, forgiveness and peace. Amen

Building a strong family

■ Take a moment to think about the qualities you would like to see in your family. How would you like to be able to describe your family?

Colossians 3:12-17

12 As God's chosen ones, holy and beloved, clothe yourselves with compassion, kindness, humility, meekness, and patience. 13 Bear with one another and, if anyone has a complaint against another, forgive each other; just as the Lord has forgiven you, so you also must forgive. 14 Above all, clothe yourselves with love, which binds everything together in perfect harmony. 15 And let the peace of Christ rule in your hearts, to which indeed you were called in the one body. And be thankful. 16 Let the word of Christ dwell in you richly; teach and admonish one another in all wisdom; and with gratitude in your hearts sing psalms, hymns, and spiritual songs to God. 17 And whatever you do, in word or deed, do everything in the name of the Lord Jesus, giving thanks to God the Father through him.

Paul's letter to the Colossians describes the essential qualities of a Christian family, as well as the Christian community.

■ How do your hopes for your family life fit with this Scripture passage?

■ What would it be like if this Scripture passage was lived out in your family?

Read the eight characteristics of strong families and discuss the questions.

All families have strengths, and families become even stronger by discovering and building on their particular strengths. Strong families are not problem-free, but learn to harness their resources to overcome difficulties.

The following characteristics of a strong family are identified in the research and writings of Nick Stinnett and John De-Frain, researchers and authors on the dynamics of families:

    a. The family shares a sense of commitment and connectedness.
    b. The family spends both quality and quantity time together, sharing many areas of life.
    c. The family engages in communication that is clear, open, honest, and frequent.
    d. Family members appreciate one another and take the time to let one another know this in a variety of ways.

e. The family has clearly defined roles for each member.
f. The family has a shared religious and moral core.
g. The family is involved in the community.
h. The family is able to cope with crisis and times of stress in a positive manner.

■ Which of these characteristics do you see in your family now?

■ Which characteristics would you like to develop in your family?

A further look

Form teams and divide the eight asset categories.

Developing a family that promotes growth

The 40 assets from Search Institute provide the building blocks that help children start out well and grow up to be healthy, well adjusted, and strong.

Together with your team, review the assets in your category Then, on the lines provided, suggest ways in which families with young children can put these assets into practice. (Turn to pages 52-53 for a list of the assets.)

a. Support: 1, 2, 6
b. Empowerment: 7-10
c. Boundaries and Expectations: 11, 14, 15, 16
d. Constructive Use of Time: 17-20
e. Commitment to Learning: 21-25
f. Positive Values: 26-31
g. Social Competencies: 32-36
h. Positive Identity: 37-40

_____

_____

_____

_____

_____

_____

■ How can you strengthen these assets in your family?

■ What new thing would you like to start doing to nurture the growth of your child?

Effective parenting

Develop a list of the characteristics of effective parenting.

Effective parenting is learned. We learn how to be effective parents by developing an understanding of our growing children. We also become effective parents by learning from other parents, parenting books and courses, and our own parenting experiences.

While there is no definitive list of effective parenting practices, the following suggestions provide helpful insights. This list is based on the book *Back to the Family* by Ray Guarendi (New York: Villard Books, 1990).

Give love unconditionally. Unconditional love is unaffected by misbehavior or disobedience.

Communicate your love and affection in words and actions.

Teach through your example. Model the faith and values you want your child to adopt.

Spend time with your child. By investing quantity time, which is necessary for quality time, you foster your child's self-esteem and sense of belonging.

Listen before you speak. Become aware of your child's "prime times" to talk and arrange to be present at those times.

Parent in the present. When we second-guess ourselves and fear the future, it is difficult to give our best in the present.

Expect that your child will misunderstand and even claim to dislike you at times. This is a reality of responsible parenthood.

Laugh whenever and wherever you can during child rearing. Humor helps maintain perspective and eases anxiety.

Allow children to have a voice in family decisions, whenever possible.

The family home is everyone's home, so make it everyone's responsibility, including your preschooler.

Expect children to live up to their capabilities—social, emotional, and personal.

Use discipline that is motivated by unconditional love. Focus most on what your child does right and emphasize the positive. Effective discipline is marked by calmness, consistency, and consequences. Consequences, not words, are the basic tools of discipline.

- Are any of these practices already at work in your family? If so, will you continue them?

- What new practices will you begin in your family?

Distribute sheets of paper and pens or pencils for this activity. When everyone has completed the sentences, share your ideas.

Consider this

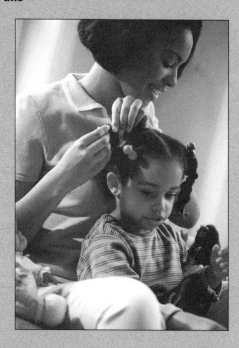

Personal parenting creed

Develop personal parenting creeds by completing statements such as "I believe parents of young children . . ." or "As a parent of young children, I will . . ."

A further look

Baptism connection

In Baptism, we are reborn by water and the Holy Spirit. This Spirit brings blessings or fruits to our lives. As Paul writes in Galatians, "the fruit of the Spirit is love, joy, peace, patience, kindness, generosity, faithfulness, gentleness, and self-control" (5:22-23).

- How has the Holy Spirit blessed your family with these fruits?

- Take a moment for prayer. Reflect on which of these fruits your family most needs now. Pray to the Holy Spirit to respond to your needs.

Wrap-up

Before you go, take time for the following:

- Group ministry task

- Review

- Personal concerns and prayer concerns

- Closing prayers

Daily walk

Bible readings

Day 1
Romans 12:9-13

Day 2
John 15:12-17

Day 3
1 Corinthians 13:1-13

Day 4
Luke 6:37-38

Day 5
Philippians 2:1-11

Day 6
Ephesians 4:1-6

Day 7
Deuteronomy 6:1-9

Verse for the journey

Love is patient; love is kind; love is not envious or boastful or arrogant or rude. It does not insist on its own way; it is not irritable or resentful; it does not rejoice in wrongdoing, but rejoices in the truth. It bears all things, believes all things, hopes all things, endures all things. 1 Corinthians 13:4-7

Thought for the journey

Effective parenting is an attainable reality. Build upon the essentials, and no level of family success is beyond your reach.

Prayer for the journey

Gracious God, thank you for the gift of our children. Guide us in raising our children to live and grow in faith each day. In Jesus' name we pray. Amen

Appendix

Group directory

Record information about group members here.

Names	Addresses	Phone numbers

Prayers

■ Closing Prayer

Lord God, you have called your servants
to ventures of which we cannot see the
ending, by paths as yet untrodden,
through perils unknown. Give us faith to
go out with good courage, not knowing
where we go, but only that your hand is
leading us and your love supporting us;
through Jesus Christ our Lord. Amen

From *Lutheran Book of Worship* (page 153) copyright © 1978.

(If you plan to pray the Lord's Prayer, record the
version your group uses in the next column.)

■ The Lord's Prayer

Group commitments

Do not be conformed to this world, but be transformed by the renewing of your minds, so that you may discern what is the will of God—what is good and acceptable and perfect. Romans 12:2

■ For our time together, we have made the following commitments to each other

■ Goals for our study of this topic are

■ Our group ministry task is

■ My personal action plan is

Prayer requests

_____

_____

_____

_____

_____

_____

_____

_____

_____

_____

_____

40 Developmental Assets for Preschoolers

EXTERNAL ASSETS

ASSET TYPE	ASSET NAME	ASSET DEFINITION
Support	1. Family support	Family life provides high levels of love and support.
	2. Positive family communication	Parents and preschoolers communicate positively. Preschoolers seek out parents for help with difficult tasks or situations.
	3. Other adult relationships	Preschoolers have support from at least one adult other than their parents. Their parents have support from people outside the home.
	4. Caring neighborhood	Preschoolers experience caring neighbors.
	5. Caring out-of-home climate	Preschoolers are in caring, encouraging environments outside the home.
	6. Parent involvement in out-of-home situations	Parents are actively involved in helping preschoolers succeed in situations outside the home. Parents communicate preschoolers' needs to caretakers outside the home.
Empowerment	7. Community values children	Parents and other adults in the community value and appreciate preschoolers.
	8. Children are given useful roles	Parents and other adults create ways preschoolers can help out and gradually include preschoolers in age-appropriate tasks.
	9. Service to others	The family serves others in the community together.
	10. Safety	Preschoolers have safe environments at home, in out-of-home settings, and in the neighborhood. This includes childproofing these environments.
Boundaries and Expectations	11. Family boundaries	The family has clear rules and consequences. The family monitors preschoolers and consistently demonstrates appropriate behavior through modeling and limit setting.
	12. Out-of-home boundaries	Childcare settings and other out-of-home environments have clear rules and consequences to protect preschoolers while consistently providing appropriate stimulation and enough rest.
	13. Neighborhood boundaries	Neighbors take responsibility for monitoring and supervising preschoolers' behavior as they begin to play and interact outside the home.
	14. Adult role models	Parents and other adults model positive, responsible behavior.
	15. Positive peer interactions	Preschoolers are encouraged to play and interact with other children in safe, well-supervised settings.
	16. Appropriate expectations for growth	Adults have realistic expectations for preschoolers' development at this age. Parents, caregivers, and other adults encourage preschoolers to achieve and develop their unique talents.
Constructive Use of Time	17. Creative activities	Preschoolers participate in music, art, dramatic play, or other creative activities each day.
	18. Out-of-home activities	Preschoolers interact in stimulating ways with children outside the family. The family keeps preschoolers' needs in mind when attending events.
	19. Religious community	The family regularly attends religious programs or services while keeping preschoolers' needs in mind.
	20. Positive, supervised time at home	Preschoolers are supervised by an adult at all times. Preschoolers spend most evenings and weekends at home with their parents in predictable, enjoyable routines.

Reprinted with permission from Search Institute, *Starting Out Right: Developmental Assets for Children* © 1997 Search Institute, Minneapolis, MN. www.search-institute.org

INTERNAL ASSETS

ASSET TYPE	ASSET NAME	ASSET DEFINITION
Commitment to Learning	21. Achievement expectation and motivation	Parents and other adults convey and reinforce expectations to do well at work, at school, in the community, and within the family.
	22. Children are engaged in learning	Parents and family members model responsive and attentive attitudes at work, at school, in the community, and at home.
	23. Stimulating activity	Parents encourage preschoolers to explore and provide stimulating toys that match preschoolers' emerging skills. Parents are sensitive to preschoolers' dispositions, preferences, and level of development.
	24. Enjoyment of learning	Parents and other adults enjoy learning and engage preschoolers in learning activities.
	25. Reading for pleasure	Adults read to preschoolers for at least 30 minutes over the course of a day, encouraging preschoolers to participate.
Positive Values	26. Family values caring	Preschoolers are encouraged to express sympathy for someone who is distressed and begin to develop a variety of helping behaviors.
	27. Family values equality and social justice	Parents place a high value on promoting social equality, religious tolerance, and reducing hunger and poverty while modeling these beliefs for preschoolers.
	28. Family values integrity	Parents act on their convictions, stand up for their beliefs, and communicate and model this in the family.
	29. Family values honesty	Preschoolers learn the difference between telling the truth and lying.
	30. Family values responsibility	Preschoolers learn that their actions affect other people.
	31. Family values healthy lifestyle	Parents and other adults model, monitor, and teach the importance of good health habits. Preschoolers begin to learn healthy sexual attitudes and beliefs as well as respect for others.
Social Competencies	32. Planning and decision making practice	Preschoolers begin to make simple choices, solve simple problems, and develop simple plans at age-appropriate levels.
	33. Interpersonal interactions	Preschoolers play and interact with other children and adults. They freely express their feelings and learn to put these feelings into words. Parents and other adults model and teach empathy.
	34. Cultural interactions	Preschoolers are exposed in positive ways to information about and to people of different cultural, racial, and/or ethnic backgrounds.
	35. Resistance practice	Preschoolers are taught to resist participating in inappropriate or dangerous behavior.
	36. Peaceful conflict resolution practice	Parents and other adults model positive ways to resolve conflicts. Preschoolers are taught and begin to practice nonviolent, acceptable ways to deal with challenging and frustrating situations.
Positive Identity	37. Family has personal power	Parents feel they have control over things that happen in their own lives and model coping skills, demonstrating healthy ways to deal with frustrations and challenges. Parents respond to preschoolers so preschoolers begin to learn that they have influence over their immediate surroundings.
	38. Family models high self-esteem	Parents create an environment where preschoolers can develop positive self-esteem, giving preschoolers appropriate, positive feedback and reinforcement about their skills and competencies.
	39. Family has a sense of purpose	Parents report that their lives have purpose and model these beliefs through their behaviors. Preschoolers are curious and explore the world around them.
	40. Family has a positive view of the future	Parents are hopeful and positive about their personal future and work to provide a positive future for children.

Resources

Books

The Classic Treasury of Children's Prayers. Minneapolis: Augsburg, 2000.

Caldwell, Elizabeth. *Making a Home for Faith.* Cleveland: United Church Press, 2000.

Chesto, Kathleen. *Raising Kids Who Care— About Themselves, About Their World, About Each Other.* Kansas City, Mo.: Sheed and Ward, 1996.

Coffey, Kathy. *Experiencing God with Your Children.* New York: Crossroad Publishing, 1998.

Dosick, Wayne. *Golden Rules—The Ten Ethical Values Parents Need to Teach Their Children.* San Francisco: HarperSanFrancisco, 1995.

Finley, Mitch and Kathy. *Building Christian Families.* Allen, Texas: Thomas More/Tabor, 1996.

Fitzpatrick, Jean Grasso. *Small Wonder— How to Answer Your Child's Impossible Questions About Life.* New York: Viking, 1994.

————, Jean Grasso. *Something More—Nurturing your Child's Spiritual Growth.* New York: Viking, 1991.

Klug, Ron and Lyn. *Jesus Lives! The Story of Jesus for Children.* Minneapolis: Augsburg, 1982.

McGrath, Tom. *Raising Faith-Filled Kids.* Chicago: Loyola Press, 2000.

Nelson, Gertrud Mueller. *To Dance with God—Family Ritual and Community Celebration.* New York: Paulist Press, 1986.

Nolte, Dorothy Law. *Children Learn What They Live.* New York: Workman Publishing, 1998.

O'Neal, Debbie Trafton. *I Can Pray with Jesus: The Lord's Prayer for Children.* Minneapolis: Augsburg, 1997.

————. *Thank You for This Day: Action Prayers, Songs, and Blessings for Every Day.* Minneapolis: Augsburg, 2000.

Payden, Deborah Alberswerth, and Laura Loving. *Celebrating at Home—Prayers and Liturgies for Families.* Cleveland: United Church Press, 1998.

Roehlkepartain, Jolene, and Nancy Leffert. *What Young Children Need to Succeed.* Minneapolis: Free Spirit Publishing, 2000.

Web sites

See the Center for Ministry Development's Web site at http://cmdnet.org for more resources for parents and children.

See the Search Institute's Web site at http://www.search-institute.org for more information on the 40 developmental assets for growth.

Please tell us about your experience with INTERSECTIONS.

4. What I like best about my INTERSECTIONS experience is

5. Three things I want to see the same in future INTERSECTIONS books are

6. Three things I might change in future INTERSECTIONS books are

7. Topics I would like developed for new INTERSECTIONS books are

8. Our group had _____ sessions for the six chapters of this book.

9. Other comments I have about INTERSECTIONS are

Thank you for taking the time to fill out and return this questionnaire.

- FOLD CARD IN HERE, SEAL WITH TAPE, AND MAIL TODAY! -

Name _____

Address _____

Daytime telephone _____

Please check the INTERSECTIONS book you are evaluating.

☐ The Bible and Life	☐ Parenting	☐ Parenting: Raising Faithful Older Adolescents
☐ Caring and Community	☐ Parenting: Raising Faithful Preschoolers	
☐ Death and Grief		☐ Peace
☐ Faith	☐ Parenting: Raising Faithful Grade-schoolers	☐ Praying
☐ Following Jesus		☐ Reconcilable Differences
☐ Integrity	☐ Parenting: Raising Faithful Younger Adolescents	☐ Smart Choices
☐ Jesus: Divine and Human		
☐ Managing Stress		

Please tell us about your small group.

1. Our group had an average attendance of _____.

2. Our group was made up of
    _____ Young adults (19-25 years).
    _____ Adults (most between 25-45 years).
    _____ Adults (most between 45-60 years).
    _____ Adults (most between 60-75 years).
    _____ Adults (most 75 and over).
    _____ Adults (wide mix of ages).
    _____ Men (number) and _____ women (number).

3. Our group (answer as many as apply)
    _____ came together for the sole purpose of studying this INTERSECTIONS book.
    _____ has decided to study another INTERSECTIONS book.
    _____ is an ongoing Sunday school group.
    _____ met at a time other than Sunday morning.
    _____ had only one facilitator for this study.

BUSINESS REPLY MAIL

FIRST-CLASS MAIL   PERMIT NO. 22120   MINNEAPOLIS, MN

POSTAGE WILL BE PAID BY ADDRESSEE

Augsburg Fortress

ATTN INTERSECTIONS TEAM
PO BOX 1209
MINNEAPOLIS MN 55440-8807